Other Titles by Christie Jones Ray

Eliza (2012)

Eliza and a Cottage Door (2012)

Eliza Has a Cousin (2012)

Eliza Celebrates a Royal Wedding (2012)

Eliza at Rose Water Cottage (2017)

Pick a Pick a Pumpkin (2012)

Here We Go a' Gathering (2012)

Goat's Milk and Gardening (2013)

Eliza Meets Ella Grace Louise (2015)

Eliza Visits Martha's Vineyard (2014)

Eliza Visits the Ballet (2016)

Eliza Will Not be Afraid (2012)

A Mouse-Making Guide (2012)

The Fox Family of Franklin (2012)

Baby Mouse with Rosebud and Sugarlump (2017)

Lula Kate Meets Eliza (2018)

More adventures of Eliza and friends
coming soon
www.christiejonesray.com

Come...all who
are weary, and I
will give you rest.
Matthew 11:28

Eliza Visits
THE PRAIRIE

story · illustrations · calligraphy ·
by: Christie Jones Ray

Rose Water Cottage Press

Pleasant View, Jennessee

This book is dedicated to the little children who attended Story time at Round Top Family Library and welcomed Eliza the mouse with open hearts . You are precious in His sight.

Rose Water Cottage Press
Franklin, Tennessee 37064
copyright ©2016 by Christie Jones Ray
Second Edition
ISBN 978-9961393-6-6
Library of Congress Control Number : 2015960948
10 9 8 7 6 5 4 3 2 1
Printed in the United States of America

About Eliza

Eliza is a very tiny, very loved, handmade toy mouse who resides at Grammy's House in the country. She wears a hand-knitted shawl and a kerchief. She has many adventures but is always happy to return home and snuggle into her cozy bed, that is actually a very lovely soap dish.

On a chilly morning in April
in the little cottage of white
Eliza peeks into Grammy's room.
She discovers boots ...
Cowboy boots
and a bag...
a traveling bag...
sitting alongside the white
ruffled bedskirt of the big bed
... and she wonders.
Grammy bustles about
in and out of the bedroom . . .
to the laundry room...
back and forth... back and forth .
Finally, she scoops up mousie.

The dresser is terribly old . . .
and one of the tiny drawer knobs
is missing.

She gently places Eliza atop
the mousie-sized dresser
arranging her next to the palest
petals of two fading blooms
and carefully opens the drawers.
Each one has been lined with tiny strips
of fragile old wallpaper.
Faded roses in soft pinks mingle with
the soft blues of the morning glories
and hydrangeas,
reminding Grammy of the papered
walls of the farmhouse where her
grandparents lived.
She loved visits there, as a little girl.

Eliza's knitted and crocheted shawls
and kerchief, along with her softest
loved~ on handkersniffs,
are tucked neatly inside these drawers.
She gazes into the ancient mirror
watching Grammy's reflection
as she slips the tiny crown over her

mousie ears

and ties the tiny tutu 'round her

mousie middle.
And Grammy whispers . . .

"We are traveling to a place that has
been inspired by old farmhouses with
their friendly porches and flower-y
old wallpaper... and little houses on
the prairie,
with their cozy hearths and
farm tables...
where roses and ivy climb up
and over and through the
picket fences...
and where pretty china and mason jars
and cloth napkins
make you feel special and right
at home."

"We will snuggle into a big
comfy bed
with down-filled covers
and down-filled pillows,
and our sleep will be sweet."
Eliza's little mousie
heart beats fast,
and she can hardly wait
for the adventure to
begin.

A thimble~ful of Lavender Wash in
a lusterware tea cup... a mousie's
way of laundering.

"Now it is time to prepare. We must
launder our clothes & pajamas
and handkersniffs
and shawls and kerchiefs,
for it has been
a Long Winter,
and we must freshen our
wardrobe for spring
and the warmth of Texas.
Yes! We will be traveling
to that very big state
with its' wide open spaces
blanketed with Bluebonnets
as far as the eye can see."

Eliza ponders, "Blue bonnets.
Why, I LOVE bonnets!
And blue IS that heavenly hue."
Grammy smiles and says,
"Little Eliza, Bluebonnets are tiny
flowers that grow across the fields in
Texas.
They will be all a'bloom just in
time for our visit.
We will gather tiny petals in
your tiny basket
and press them between the
pages of your tiny book."
She tries so very hard to imagine
that blanket of blue.

Eliza loves to wear her tiny crown
and her shimmering tutu and her
ballet slippers...with their tiny pink ribbon ties...
But she wonders
Is this what others will be wearing?
Will they think it's strange
that I'm dressed this way?
What about my crown
with its wonderful sparkles?
Oh –
will I fit in
in Texas?

Grammy twirls the mousie's tail
...that long, soft
cotton wicking tail...
and reassures
her anxious mousie mind.
"Yes, little Eliza, you'll fit in.
Be yourself and no one else,
and they'll love
You
for being You."

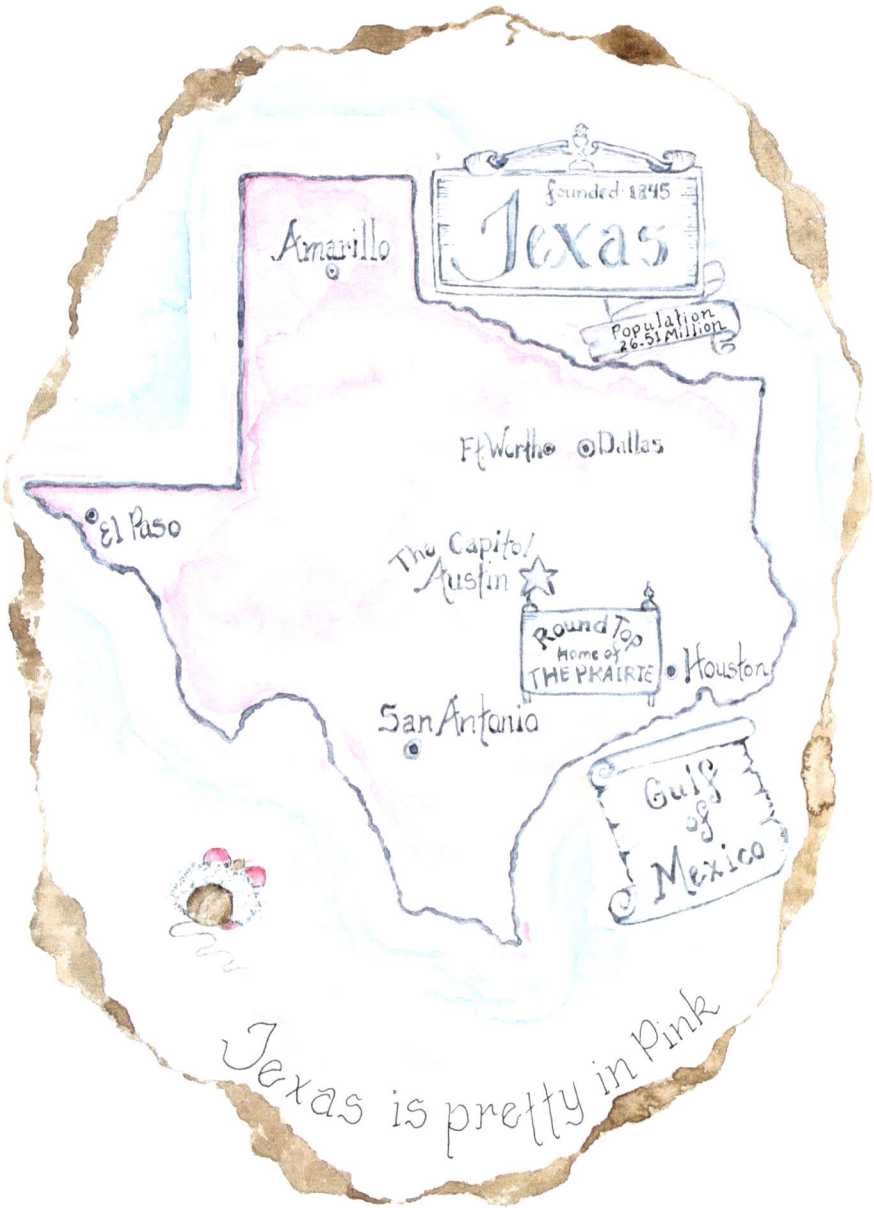

Amarillo

Founded 1845
Jexas

Population
26.51 Million

Ft Worth Dallas

El Paso

The Capitol
Austin

Round Top
Home of
THE PRAIRIE Houston

San Antonio

Gulf
of
Mexico

Jexas is pretty in Pink

Packing and preparations continue
and in the blink of an eye...it is time
to board that very big plane
and fly to that very
big state.

The sun is warm,
and the wind is blowing as they
make their way to
The Prairie by Rachel Ashwell
...the inspired place.

Along the way, there are cows and
ponies and donkeys.
There are cows with long horns
and cows with long ears.
There are cows with curls
atop their heads.
There are calves...
calves that are romping & nuzzling
and butting heads & wandering.
There are brown ones & tan ones
and even white ones
with pink ears and pink noses.

Beyond the fences, lie blankets
and blankets
of b l u e.
Grammy plucks a tiny bonnet
with its petals of that
vivid Heavenly Hue.
Eliza's basket has never
looked sweeter.

The Prairie

The winding roads go on and on... but at last, there is found... a white wooden sign... with blue painted letters... attached to an old wooden fence, and they turn there.

The long gravel drive leads them
straight to the very old house,
and it is beautiful
with its weathered white siding
and pale blue door.
A family once called this
Home
long, long ago.

They follow the drive
as it winds along to the left,
and they come upon
the tiny barn
that will serve as their
~ Home away from Home ~

The gate is propped open against
the white picket fence.
A wooden sign
with chipping paint
reads

Eliza scoots in 'neath the lovely bouquet, alongside
the leather notebook, atop this table of
bright green ... surely this is a dream.

Grammy and Eliza follow the
flagstone path to the
French door entry . . .
and with a turn of the key,
they enter the
Blue Bonnet Barn
with its fresh white walls
and inviting brick floors...
charming little windows with
lace panel curtains.
It is quite a magical cottage
indeed.

A dainty, mousie~sized crown ♡

Grammy carries their traveling bags
to the cozy bedroom and begins
to unpack.
Eliza's bed is first
with its soft cotton hanky...
followed by a dainty crown
of velvet~y flowers...
then her tiny basket of
Bluebonnets
...and finally, her
little book.
Gingerly, they are arranged
atop the old pink dresser,
and mousie girl is snuggled into the
soft pink slippers.

The petals of blue have begun to
wilt…just a bit…and they
are tenderly pressed
between the pages of one
mousie-sized book.
A pink ribbon, wrapped
around a crisp white
wash cloth, is found on the bench
alongside the clawfoot tub.
It is just the right length,
and Grammy fastens it round
the tattered cover,
keeping the fragile petals
inside.

From the dresser, the tiny mouse
sees the big bed with its comfy
cover and pillows.
The pretty posey print reminds
Eliza of the pink wildflowers
sprinkled along the roadways.
A dream catcher hangs on the
wall...above the bed.
Only sweet dreams
will come to the one who
lies beneath
that beautiful web.

Eliza loves the scent of Grapefruit

Oh, if only Grammy had packed the
mousie-sized tub

Grammy retreats to the bath
and as the hot water pours from
the faucet...and splashes
against the old stopper
covering the drain...
frothy bubbles begin to form.
The fragrance wafts
through the air...quite a
delicious fragrance, indeed.

After a time, and refreshed from
her bath...she reappears, wearing
her long white nightgown.
Pulling back the feather-filled
covers and fluffing the big
mushy pillows...
slipping off her slippers
and crawling into bed,
she softly whispers to
Eliza...

"At last, we shall snuggle into a big comfy bed, and our sleep will be sweet."

Eliza remembers the verse stitched 'round the edges of her handkersniff...

"He will cover you with His feathers... and under His wings you will find refuge." Psalm 91:4

Bright and early the following morning, Grammy pulls on her bluejeans and cowboy boots...
for that is what all the ladies wear at The Prairie...

unless you are a mouse named Eliza.

Oh how she loves her slippers of pink.

Once again, she is scooped up
into those gentle hands
and whisked away for a very special
s u r p r i s e.
Across the way, stands a
lovely white barn
with wide wooden steps...
leading to its wide wooden porch.

The sound of Grammy's boots
as she makes her way across
the wide plank floors
is all that can be heard . . .
along with the 'coo' of
the Mourning Dove
and the 'caw' of
the Blue Jay.

Eliza believes the barn is
quite lovely...with its flower-y
papered walls
and the farm table with its chipping
pink paint... My goodness!
It is the l o n g e s t table she has
ever seen!
The very large barrels
filled with silk
roses and wisteria and larkspur
and dogwood blossoms
is beautiful, as well ...
And she wonders ...

Why would Grammy bring her
into this barn... so early in
the morning, while the grass
is still wet with the morning dew.
She is lifted high,
and with her glass~beaded eyes
she beholds the dresses...
the array of pastel prom dresses.
They appear to be dancing about
in the rafters of the
great Pearl Barn.

The fulle ruffles
and the ribbon sashes
and the lace trims...
are in the sweetest softest shades
of **lilacs** & **pinks**
and **blues**.

She has never seen such a
display,
And she thinks...

There had been a wonderful celebration...
the World of Shabby Chic had turned

25

How wonderful it is
to visit a place
...a little piece of heaven...
where girls can be girlie,
and tutus and crowns
and slippers of pink
can be worn and tied 'round
fat mousie middles
and w i d e mousie feet
and BIG mousie ears
·It truly is so nice to have that little bit of bling·
...And she fits in.

The two leave the roominess
of the great barn
and make their way to the coziness.
of the Ranger's Lounge
where the smells of
breakfast and fresh coffee
greet the hungry guests.
...along with a kitty named Pearlie
who's yawning & stretching.

Pitchers of roses and mason jar vases
are aligned center stage the length
of another farm table.
The blooms of whites & pinks & lavenders
with their sleepy velvet heads, nod a soft
'Good Morning'
Rumple-y cloth napkins, wrappings
for mismatched forks & spoons & knives,
find their place alongside
the pretty prairie dishes.

Round Top Family Library

Breakfast is a feast
and will carry them through
their day as they explore the town
that is Round Top
with its charming shops
and cafes
and Library...its wonderfully enchanting
Library.

. The · Story · Time · Hour .

12 1 2 3 4 5 6 7 8 9 10 11

Little hand on the 10... the tale begins .

Little hand on the tail... the mouse will spin ♡

Grammy will sit upon a chair
amongst the little children, there
at the Story Time Hour.
She will read her little books
and she will answer many many
questions...
and Eliza will twirl ...
round and round ...
hanging upside down ...
... being held by the end
of her cotton wicking tail.

They will taste pie
the very best PIE...
and they will sip tea...
the sweetest TEA tasted.

They will find treasures
...the most special
remembrances
of their adventure.

BORN & DIED
APRIL 9 1885
AT REST

They will pause in a cemetery
with sun-dappled markers
and stacked stone walls. . .
and they will linger. . .
thinking thoughtfully
of those who
lived and died, here
over one hundred years ago.

Rest has been plenty...
inspiration, too...
and the time
has come
for Grammy and
her little mousie friend
to say their Goodbyes
to this haven and all that is
lovely and Shabby and Chic.

Goodbye comfy bed, comfy covers and pillows . . .
big squashy sofa and fragrant fruit bubbles.
Goodbye to the cows and Pearl pup & Pearl kitty.
Goodbye fancy dresses that dance through the rafters.
Farewell to the pickeled fences and roses . . .
   and ivy that winds over arbors & railings.
Best wishes to ladies who wash mousie dishes
and make all things special and make all things
                        pretty.
A bow to the man in the big boots and
     hat, for all that he does . . .
   and doesn't mind aprons.

All blessings and love
to the shy British lady,
who dreamed a big dream
and prayed it would happen.
Farewell to

THE PRAIRIE

with all of our
Love ~
Grammy &
Eliza the mouse.

About the Author/Illustrator

Christie Jones Ray is a former teacher who began writing a blog in 2011, sharing stories of her handmade mouse, named after her four-foot-tall great grandmother.

Her grandson had so many adventures with the toy mouse that her husband encouraged her to write a children's book. It took much convincing, but by summer's end, she had written the text that would become material for a series of books about Eliza the mouse at Grammy's House.

She is a self-taught artist who only began drawing and working with watercolors in the fall of 2011, at the age of fifty.

Acknowledgements

- Rachel Pallas...who created & gifted Eliza with the most darling, miniature floral crown. www.etsy.com/shop/shabbyforme
- Jolie Sikes-Smith of the Junk Gypsies... who designed & created (with daddy Phil's help) the lighted marquis for the celebration of 25 years of Shabby Chic. It is a permanent fixture in the Pearl Barn at The Prairie by Rachel Ashwell. Junk Gypsies/GAC hosts: Amie Sikes & Jolie Sikes-Smith Season 3, Episode 5 - 25th Anniversary party for Shabby Chic.
- Lizzie Lou's Antiques & Vintage... purveyors of unique treasures, where I acquired the beloved cow pitcher. 107 Main Street Round Top, Texas.
- Royer's Round Top Cafe...home of the very best pies and sweetest tea tasted. We love you Pieman, Bud Royer. 105 Main Street Round Top, Texas.
- Round Top Family Library's Barbara Smith, Director and her assistant extraordinaire, Mary Leitko, who allowed me to read my little books to the pre-schoolers at Story time and share my paints with the budding artists in their after school program. What a magical place. 206 W. Mill Street Round Top, Texas.
- The Little Cowgirl - Diann Rigsby & corgi Charles Francis, who showed me Texas and where the Bluebonnets grow.   Sugar Tree, Tennessee
- Kelly and Jeresa Nielsen of Studio 92, LLC, the designers of the book. I am forever grateful for your amazing skills and your enduring patience on each and every project I send your way.

⌐ The Shabby Chic Team... Jaimee Seabury,
Sarah Pankow, and Kelly DiNisco...
and those who keep The Prairie by Rachel Ashwell
spit spot... and the guests well-fed & tended to...
Daniel Riebeling · Kim Alley Wimberly · Kathy Zingelmann
along with Kim Mercer Thweatt, coordinator of events, there.

⌐ and Finally...
Rachel Ashwell... creator of the Shabby Chic
aesthetic, who had the vision for this lovely respite
in the peaceful prairie of Round Top, Texas.
Thank you for pouring love and demonstrating
the "beauty of imperfection" in every detail...
and for your blessing on my efforts to relay
the magic that is The Prairie by Rachel Ashwell.

www.ingramcontent.com/pod-product-compliance
Lightning Source LLC
Chambersburg PA
CBHW040942100426
42813CB00018B/2899